D1709139

WITHDRAWN

Maya Lin

Jefferson Madison
Regional Library
Charlottesville, Virginia

30935 8933
C

Published in the United States of America by Cherry Lake Publishing
Ann Arbor, Michigan
www.cherrylakepublishing.com

Reading Adviser: Marla Conn, MS, Ed, Literacy Specialist, Read-Ability, Inc.
Book Designer: Jennifer Wahi
Illustrator: Jeff Bane

Photo Credits: © tab62/Shutterstock.com, 5; © Forge Mind Archives/Flickr, 7, 13, 22; © Sharon VanderKaay/Flickr, 9; © KelseyJ/Shutterstock.com, 11; © LEE SNIDER PHOTO IMAGES / Shutterstock.com, 15, 19, 21; © Zack Frank/Shutterstock.com, 17, 23; Cover, 1, 6, 8, 12, Jeff Bane; Various frames throughout, ©Shutterstock Images

Copyright ©2019 by Cherry Lake Publishing
All rights reserved. No part of this book may be reproduced or utilized in any form or by any means without written permission from the publisher.

Library of Congress Cataloging-in-Publication Data

Names: Spiller, Sara, author. | Bane, Jeff, 1957- illustrator.
Title: Maya Lin / [Sara Spiller, author; Jeff Bane, illustrator].
Description: Ann Arbor, Michigan : Cherry Lake Publishing, 2019. | Series: My itty-bitty bio | Includes bibliographical references and index. | Audience: K to Grade 3.
Identifiers: LCCN 2018034510| ISBN 9781534142701 (hardcover) | ISBN 9781534140462 (pdf) | ISBN 9781534139268 (pbk.) | ISBN 9781534141667 (hosted ebook)
Subjects: LCSH: Lin, Maya Ying--Juvenile literature. | Asian American artists--Biography--Juvenile literature. | Asian American architects--Biography--Juvenile literature.
Classification: LCC N6537.L54 S65 2019 | DDC 709.2 [B] --dc23
LC record available at https://lccn.loc.gov/2018034510

Printed in the United States of America
Corporate Graphics

table of contents

My Story 4

Timeline 22

Glossary 24

Index .24

About the author: Sara Spiller is a native of the state of Michigan. She enjoys reading comic books and hanging out with her cats.

About the illustrator: Jeff Bane and his two business partners own a studio along the American River in Folsom, California, home of the 1849 Gold Rush. When Jeff's not sketching or illustrating for clients, he's either swimming or kayaking in the river to relax.

My parents were **immigrants**. They came from China. They moved to the United States. I was born in Ohio. It was 1959.

I studied at Yale University in Connecticut. I made designs.

My designs are simple.
They copy nature. My designs
look like nature.

What else have we
copied from nature?

A war had ended a few years earlier. It lasted 20 years. It was called the **Vietnam War**. Many people died.

People wanted to remember those who had died. They wanted to build a **memorial**.

There was a **contest**. The best design would become the memorial. Many people entered the contest.

I won. I had the best design. I was still in college when I won.

Have you ever won a contest?

I designed a wall. It had the names of **soldiers**. They were from the Vietnam War.

Some people did not like my design. They thought it was too simple.

Why would this make people unhappy?

But most people loved it.
They respected it.

I've made more **sculptures**.
My work is well known.

The Vietnam Veterans Memorial honors brave people.

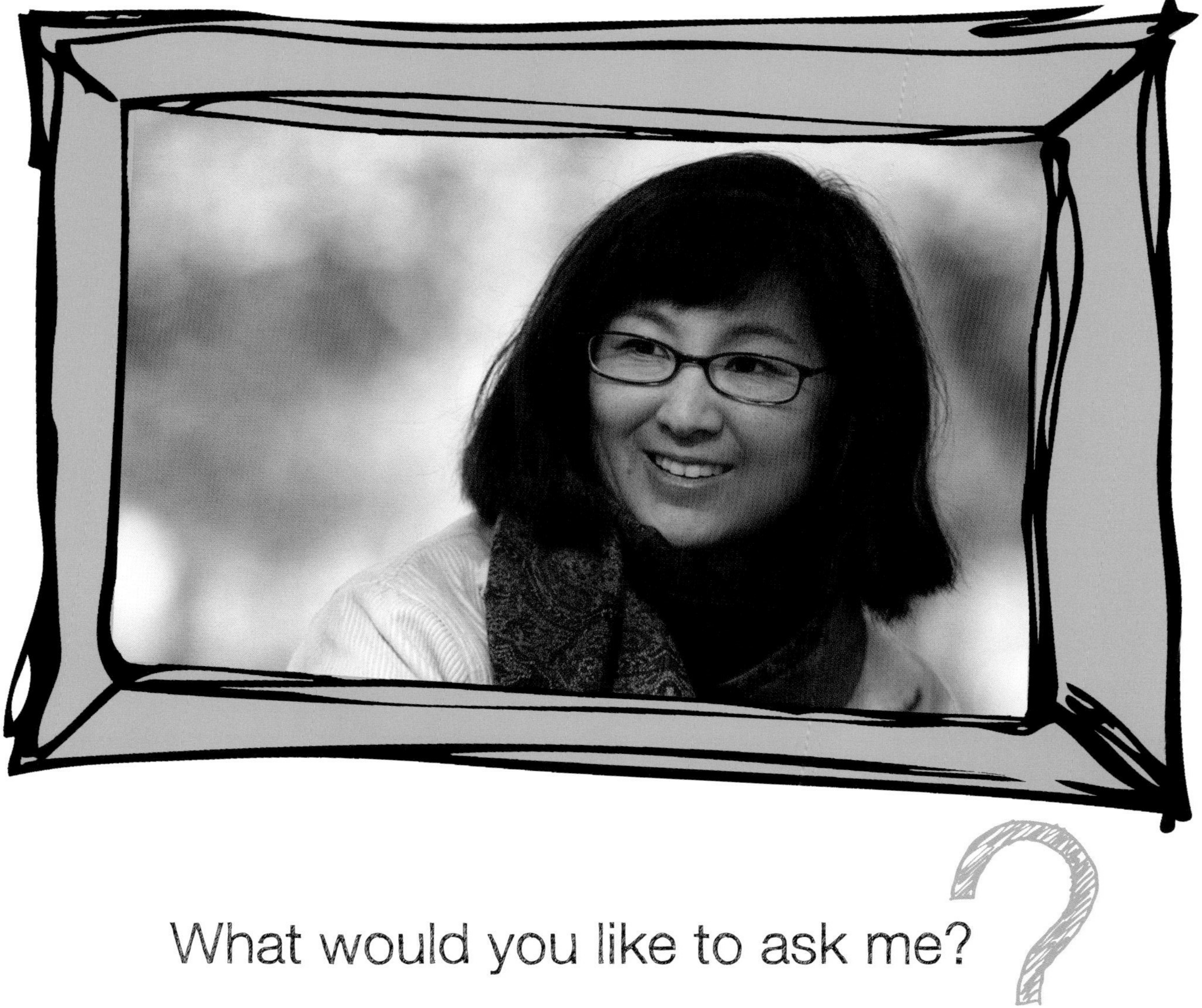

What would you like to ask me?

timeline

1981

1950

Born
1959

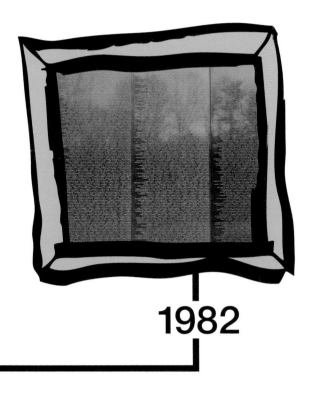

1982

2050

glossary

contest (KAHN-test) when people try to come up with an idea that is better than everyone else's

immigrants (IM-ih-gruhnts) people who move from one country to another and settle there

memorial (muh-MOR-ee-uhl) something that is built to help people remember a person or a happening

sculptures (SKUHLP-churz) things shaped out of stone, wood, clay, or metal

soldiers (SOHL-jurz) people serving in the army

Vietnam War (vee-et-NAHM WOR) a war from 1954 to 1975 between South Vietnam and North Vietnam

index

China, 4
Connecticut, 6
contest, 12, 13

design, 6, 8, 12, 14, 16

immigrants, 4

memorial, 20

nature, 8, 9

Ohio, 4

United States, 4

Vietnam War, 10, 14

Yale University, 6

24

WITHDRAWN
DEC - - 2019